A Child's First Library of Learning

Sky and Earth

TIME-LIFE BOOKS • ALEXANDRIA, VIRGINIA

Contents

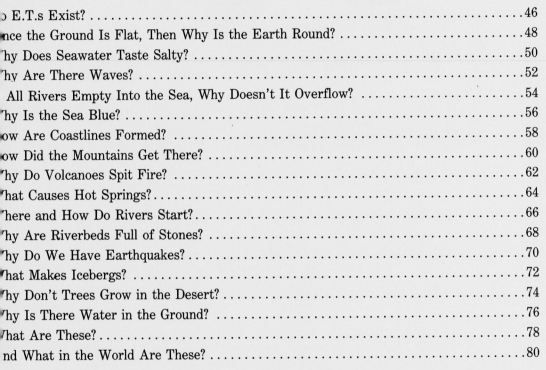

? How Was the Earth Formed?

ANSWER Our sun, the earth and eight other planets are part of the solar system. This was formed from small particles of matter scattered in space which came together with the sun, which is a star, at its center.

Gas and small particles of matter coming together formed large clumps of matter and gas. These clung together in a cloud like a swarm of mosquitos.

• To the Parent

The sun was born some five billion years ago, and the formation of the solar system was begun about the same time. The theory that is given here is the most generally held but still has not been proved conclusively. Decomposition of the radioactive substances at the earth's core generated extreme heat and volcanic activity that thrust them up to the surface. They then cooled and hardened to form the earth's crust.

The sun came into being as the nucleus of a vast cloud of small particles of matter drifting in space. Clumps of matter came together as solid spheres and became the planets, which move around the sun in elliptical orbits.

Next a ball of matter was formed. At first this ball was approximately the same on the inside as it was on the outside.

Then the ball began to heat up from the inside, melting the matter as the ball became more solid. Gas and steam from the molten center erupted to form our water and the atmosphere.

Then the crust cooled and hardened, and the continents and the oceans were formed.

Why Do We Have Day and Night?

ANSWER The earth is like a huge spinning ball, always turning in the same direction. It is daytime where we live when our part of the world is facing the sun. It is night, though, when we are turned away from the sun.

Because the earth spins from left to right, when it's early morning in the countries of Asia, it's the middle of the night in Europe, and early in the evening in the eastern United States.

Why Does the Sun Rise in the East And Set in the West?

The earth always turns towards the east, the way the arrows are pointing in the picture. If we stand facing east in the direction the earth is turning, it seems as if the sun rises in the east. At noon it seems to be right overhead. And in the evening at sunset it seems to disappear below the horizon in the west.

Ancient beliefs about day and night

The people of ancient India believed that the sun moved round a mountain at the center of the world. They thought night came when the sun was on the other side of the mountain.

● **To the Parent**

Day and night result from the rotation of the earth on its axis once every 24 hours. Living at a fixed point on the surface of the earth we may get the illusion that it is the sun that is rotating, but that is not the case. The earth revolves around the sun. It makes a complete revolution in one year. The same sort of illusion may be experienced if you are riding on a train. It may seem that the ground is flying past you, but you are the one who is moving. Even into rather recent times people incorrectly thought that the sun revolved around the earth.

How High Does the Blue Sky Go?

ANSWER The blue sky reaches only as high as the earth's atmosphere. That is the air surrounding the earth. Beyond our blue sky there is only the vast, total black darkness of outer space.

● **To the Parent**

The blue sky extends only as far as the earth's atmosphere; beyond that stretches the immeasurable blackness of outer space. While we know the universe is not infinite, we are unable to see its limits. One reason for this is that space is currently expanding at a tremendous rate, and near its outer limits is so warped that even light cannot escape. As a result, it is utterly impossible for humans to observe what the edge of the universe looks like.

How Big Is the Universe?

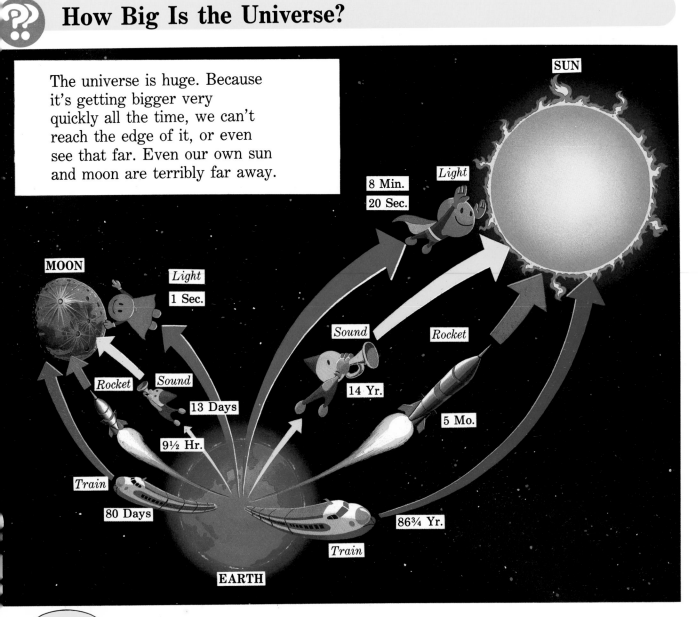

The universe is huge. Because it's getting bigger very quickly all the time, we can't reach the edge of it, or even see that far. Even our own sun and moon are terribly far away.

SUN

Light — 8 Min. 20 Sec.

MOON

Light — 1 Sec.

Sound — 14 Yr.

Rocket — 5 Mo.

Rocket — Sound — 13 Days

9½ Hr.

Train — 80 Days

Train — 86¾ Yr.

EARTH

MINI-DATA

Measuring speeds

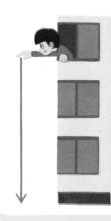

We can find out how fast something is moving by measuring how fast it travels in one second. If you drop a weight from a height of 16 feet (5 m) it will reach the ground in about one second. In seven more seconds it would travel a distance equal to the height of the Eiffel Tower.

The speed of some military planes is measured as mach. Mach one equals the speed of sound, 1,088 feet (331 m) per second. Light travels 186,000 miles (300,000 km) per second. That is about 7½ times the distance around the earth. We use light years, the distance light travels in a year, to gauge the vast reaches of space. This is such an enormous distance that even most grown-ups have trouble understanding it. A light year is 5.9 trillion miles (9.4 trillion km).

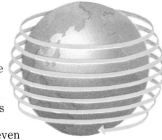

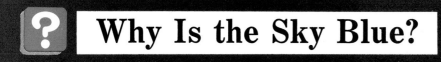

Why Is the Sky Blue?

ANSWER Light is made up of seven colors, though normally our eyes do not see the individual colors. When sunlight hits the atmosphere of the earth, however, blue breaks off from the other colors and is scattered in the air. Separated like this it becomes visible, and that is why the sky looks blue.

❓ Why Do Things Seem To Have Colors?

Ordinary light is called white light, but it is really made up of the colors red, orange, yellow, green, blue, indigo and violet. Things appear to have color because of the color of the light that is reflected back from them when white light hits them. If red light is reflected, an object will appear red.

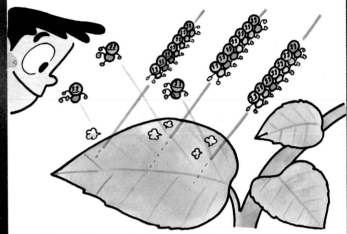

▲ Green objects reflect green light and absorb all other colors.

▲ Black objects absorb all seven colors.

MINI-DATA

Seven colors in white light

Sunlight is white light and is a mixture of seven colors. We can see the separate colors if we pass white light through a prism. They are always in the same order.

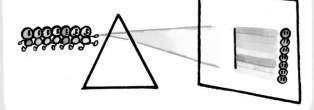

• **To the Parent**

Although it appears colorless and is referred to as white light, sunlight comprises a number of different colors. This can be proved by passing white light through a prism. Objects appear to have a certain color because that is the color of the light that they reflect. Green leaves appear green because they reflect only green light and absorb all other colors. Objects that absorb all colors appear black. The sky appears blue because blue is scattered and all other colors absorbed when sunlight enters the earth's atmosphere.

❓ How Bright Is the Sun?

ANSWER The brightness of the sun, measured in watts, is 380 followed by 24 zeros. That's brighter than all the light bulbs on earth added together. The reason the sun is so bright is that it is so incredibly hot.

MINI-DATA

Hotter means brighter

Anything will shine more brightly as it becomes hotter. The higher its temperature the brighter it shines. Watch a gas heater after it has been turned on. At first, when the fire isn't very hot, it glows a dull red color. As the fire grows hotter the color gets very much brighter.

▲ When first switched on it isn't very hot.

▲ A little later it begins to glow red.

▲ When it's hot it glows very brightly.

12

How Hot Is the Sun?

The sun is very hot indeed. It produces large amounts of heat and light at the same time. Using a magnifying glass, we can focus the heat and light of the sun at one point. Doing this makes the light very bright and the heat hot enough to start a fire.

The Sun

Magnifying glass

Heat and light from the sun's rays shining on a magnifying glass are focused on a single point.

Making electricity from the heat of the sun

The heat of the sun is called solar energy. It can be used to produce steam, which can then be turned into electricity. Here you can see an experimental solar plant. The large number of mirrors act like magnifying glasses to collect and focus solar energy to produce electricity.

If sunlight reflected from a mirror falls on your hand, you can feel the heat that is reflected with it.

▲ **A solar plant.** Here heat from the sun is turned into electricity. The circle of mirrors in the background concentrates the sun's heat on the tower in the center. In the foreground each of the many banks of mirrors catches the sun's energy.

● **To the Parent**

Temperatures on the sun range from 10,000°F. (6,000°C.) on the surface to 27 million degrees F. (15,000,000° C.) at the core. The hotter things are, the brighter, so temperatures on the sun make it dazzling. Although only a tiny fraction of its output of energy ever reaches the earth, it is enough to account for changes in climate and to sustain all animal and plant life on the planet. Generation of electricity is only one of the areas now being pursued by scientists around the world to try to find ways to harness the sun's awesome energy.

? Why Does the Sun Seem to Move?

▲ How the sun moves in a day

ANSWER Because the earth is spinning round. It is really the earth that is moving as it revolves west to east on its axis. But to people here on earth, it seems that the sun circles the earth.

The earth turns slowly, and the sun gradually comes into view. Then as the earth goes on turning, we slowly lose sight of the sun once again.

TRY THIS

The sun and shadows

You can follow the sun by watching the changes in a shadow on the ground made by a pole. Mark the first position of the shadow, then mark it twice more every half hour. The differences in the length and position of the shadows will show you exactly how the sun's position has changed.

14

The sun seems to move higher and lower too!

In the summer months, the sun rises high in the sky. In the winter months, the sun appears much lower in the sky.

For this reason, if you measure your shadow at the same time of day it will be longer in winter than it will in summer.

15

? Why Is the Sky Red at Sunset?

ANSWER Sunsets appear red because at sunset red is the only color in sunlight to reach our eyes. All the other colors are scattered before they reach us.

■ **Why the sunset looks red**

Light has farther to travel through the earth's atmosphere to reach us when the sun is low in the sky at sunset. None of the other colors travel as far as red. They are scattered before we can see them. Red travels farthest, so we can see it, and that makes the sky look red.

❓ Is That Why the Sunrise Also Seems to Be Red?

Yes, it is. Because at dawn, sunlight has to travel as far as it does at sunset, this time through the eastern sky.

▲ **Sunrise.** It is particularly beautiful in the mountains.

? Why Doesn't the Sun Set At the North Pole in Summer?

Arctic summer, our summer

ANSWER Since the earth's axis is tilted and the North Pole points towards the sun in summer, there's no sunset.

Look at the diagrams on the right. Because the earth revolves on its axis, the land at the poles doesn't have as far to go to make one complete turn as the lands where we live. In summer, the North Pole is always tilted toward the sun so there is never time for it to get really dark. Although the light is stronger at certain times and less so at others, it stays light for 24 hours. Eskimos make the most of the daylight and have no fixed time for sleeping.

Is It Dark All Day In Winter There?

Yes, because in winter the North Pole is tilted away from the sun, and the angle means sunlight can't reach it.

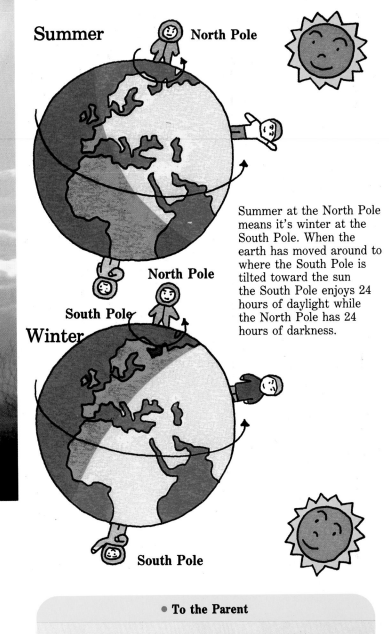

Summer at the North Pole means it's winter at the South Pole. When the earth has moved around to where the South Pole is tilted toward the sun the South Pole enjoys 24 hours of daylight while the North Pole has 24 hours of darkness.

● **To the Parent**

The invisible line running through the North and South Poles which we call the earth's axis is not perfectly vertical, but is inclined at an angle of 23½°. For that reason, as the earth orbits the sun, the North and South Poles are pointed alternately towards the sun. This, together with the earth's orbital position in relation to the sun, accounts for the seasons. During polar summers, the sun sets only partially, leaving a lingering light, and rises again while there is still light, a phenomenon that is known as the midnight sun.

Why Is the Rising Moon So Big?

ANSWER The moon only seems bigger when it first rises. Actually it is the same size when it is high in the sky. But it looks bigger when it has just risen because we compare it with buildings and objects on the horizon.

TRY THIS

Which apple is bigger?

Two apples of the same size will appear to be of different sizes if they are placed side by side on different sized plates. The apple on the smaller plate seems bigger than the apple on the larger plate. This is known as an optical illusion.

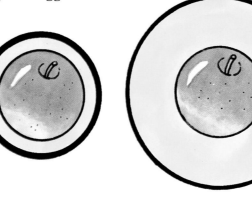

Prepare the materials in the illustration below. You will need a stick 20 inches (50 cm) long and about as thick as a pencil, a coin or token with a quarter-inch (5 mm) hole in the center and a one-inch (2.5 cm) piece of tape. Attach the coin or token to the stick as shown, taking care not to cover the hole.

Whoo! Is it true?

Try it out!

Bring one end of the stick near to your face and look at the moon through the hole in the coin. Compare the size of the moon when it is just rising to how big it is when it is higher up in the sky. You will find that the size of the moon hasn't changed, and in both cases it will be about the same size as the hole in the coin.

● To the Parent

Seen from the earth, the moon has about the same diameter as a quarter inch (5 mm) hole in a washer or coin an adult's arm length from the eye. This is smaller than you would suppose. The larger appearance of the moon when it rises is simply an optical illusion. Things appear smaller or larger depending on the size of the objects around them, and the rising moon is no exception. If an appropriately sized washer or coin is not readily available, a piece of paper with a hole in it will do.

What Is Moonlight?

ANSWER The moon catches the light of the sun and reflects it to the earth. That is what we call moonlight.

 ## Is It Dark In Outer Space?

Yes, it's totally dark in outer space, except for objects that reflect the light of the sun. That's why if you went into outer space, you would see the stars and the sun shining at the same time.

▲ **The darkness of space.** In the foreground below the spaceship is the surface of the moon. In the distance is the earth, half in light, half in darkness.

● **To the Parent**

The moon has no light of its own; it shines only with the reflected light of the sun. Although only seven percent of this reflected light reaches the earth, it makes our nights a little bit brighter. With the exception of bodies that shine with their own light, such as stars, or with reflected light, there is only total blackness in outer space beyond the blue of the earth's atmosphere. Our sun is in fact a small star, and in the blackness of space it can be seen shining together with myriad other stars scattered throughout the universe.

? Why Does the Shape Of the Moon Change?

ANSWER The moon spins around the earth. For that reason, sometimes we can see all or most of the part catching the sunlight, but sometimes we can see little or none.

The last quarter, or waning half-moon, when only the left half of the moon can be seen, appears about a week after the full moon.

At the time of the new moon, only the faint rim of the moon can be seen because it moves with the sun and is almost or completely invisible to us.

Phases of the moon

Moon

Waning Moon

Earth

Sun

New moon

● **To the Parent**

As the moon travels around the earth, the phases of the moon are determined by its position in relation to the sun and the earth. Using a light bulb for the sun and a ball as the moon, hold the ball in your hand and slowly move it in a circle around the illuminated bulb. The light on the ball will mirror the phases of the moon.

The full moon appears
perfectly round because we
are able to see one entire
side of it lit by the sun.

Full moon

Crescent moon

The waxing, or new crescent,
moon is the right-hand rim of
the moon. It appears about
three days after the new moon.

Why Is There a Moon in Daytime?

■ Full moon

When the sun sets, the full moon begins to rise in the eastern sky. At dawn, when the sun comes up, the moon sets in the west.

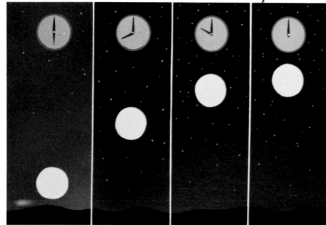

■ Crescent moon

The new crescent, or waxing moon, rises at mid-morning and stays in the sky all day long. In the evening it sets in the west. From the new moon to the full moon we say the moon is waxing.

ANSWER We see the moon in the daytime when it rises late at night and daylight comes before it can set.

The third quarter moon rises during the night, so we see it in the daytime.

First quarter moon

The first quarter moon rises about noon. By evening it is in the southern sky, and it sets at night. We see less and less of the moon after the full moon, and we say the moon is waning.

▲ **The moon in daytime**

• To the Parent

We tend to note the timing of the full moon because it rises just as the sun is setting, but we pay less attention to when the moon rises and sets in its other phases. However, if we think about the changing positions of the sun, earth and moon, it becomes obvious that moonrise will synchronize with sunset only when these are all in a straight line at the time of the full moon. During the other phases the sun will set before or after the moon rises. It is at these times that the moon will appear in the sky during the hours of daylight.

What Are the Shadows on the Moon?

ANSWER The darkish shadows on the moon are places where molten rock poured out onto its surface long ago. These areas appear darker because they do not reflect sunlight as well as others.

Why Is the Surface of the Moon so Uneven?

Like earth, the surface of the moon is made up of mountains and seas, though there is no water in the moon's seas. There are many depressions on the moon's surface called craters. These were made when meteorites hurtling through space crashed into the earth's satellite.

▲ **Craters.** They form when meteorites hit the moon.

What early people imagined about the face of the moon

▲ The Japanese thought it was a rabbit making rice cakes.

▲ Some Europeans thought it looked like a woman's face.

▲ Other Europeans thought it was shaped like a crab.

● **To the Parent**

Only the surface of the moon that reflects the sunlight is visible from earth. The moon's seas show up as darker areas. They are flat and were formed of molten lava from the moon's interior, but we don't know why. The brighter mountainous areas are pockmarked with craters that are believed to have been formed either by meteorites or by volcanic eruptions. Interpretations of the shadows on the moon have been many and varied, but space exploration has shown that there are mainly craters and few seas on the far side of the moon.

Why Do Stars Twinkle?

ANSWER Air is never still, so light passing through it is bent. When starlight points at you, you can see it. Then it bends and you can't see it, so the star appears to be twinkling.

No twinkling up here!

It looks as if the stars are twinkling from down here!

When air moves, light is bent

Something seen across a bonfire will look out of shape, because the air over the bonfire is moving and is bending the light.

Does Everything in the Universe Shine?

Stars like our sun shine with their own light. They reflect their light onto other objects, like planets or dead stars that have no light of their own, and make them shine. Black holes are a special kind of dead star. They absorb light and cannot be seen.

Stars shine by themselves. They shine brightest when they are young, but less brilliantly as they get old.

▶ Planets shine with reflected light. Like earth, the other planets in our solar system revolve around the sun and shine with its reflected light.

A black hole. This large star has collapsed into itself and become very small but powerful. Its energy is so great that it sucks everything, including light, into it, and nothing can escape.

Why Can't We See Stars During Daytime

 Stars show up clearly against the darkness of the night sky. But during the day the sunlight makes the sky so bright that it outshines the light of the stars, so we cannot see them.

87

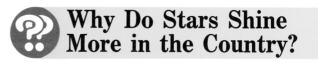

Why Do Stars Shine More in the Country?

Even at night, it is hard to see the stars where there's a lot of light. In cities the glow from street lamps and buildings lights the sky, making it hard to see even the brightest stars.

▲ **Night in the city.** The glare from the streets and the dirt in the air block out the light of the stars.

▲ **Night in the country.** The air is clear and the sky is dark, so you can see stars you can't see in the city.

Outside the earth's atmosphere. The moon is in the foreground; the sun is out of the picture; and the earth shows at the far right. Out there the sun shines just like other stars.

● **To the Parent**

Although the brightness of the daytime sky prevents us from seeing them, the stars are always visible beyond the earth's atmosphere in outer space. A total eclipse, when sunlight is temporarily blotted out, is the only time stars can be seen in the daytime. In modern cities, house and street lighting and neon signs make the low night sky so bright it is hard to see the stars from the city. And pollution compounds the problem, so that although some of its brighter stars are still visible, the Milky Way itself can hardly be seen at all.

❓ How Many Stars Are There?

ANSWER There are so many, many stars in the whole universe that we could never count them all. About 7,000 stars can be seen from the earth without a telescope, but only 2,000 of them from any one place at any one time.

No matter where we are standing, we can see something less than half of all the sky visible from earth. That is why we can see only 2,000 of the 7,000 stars that can be seen from the earth without a telescope.

▼ The Milky Way

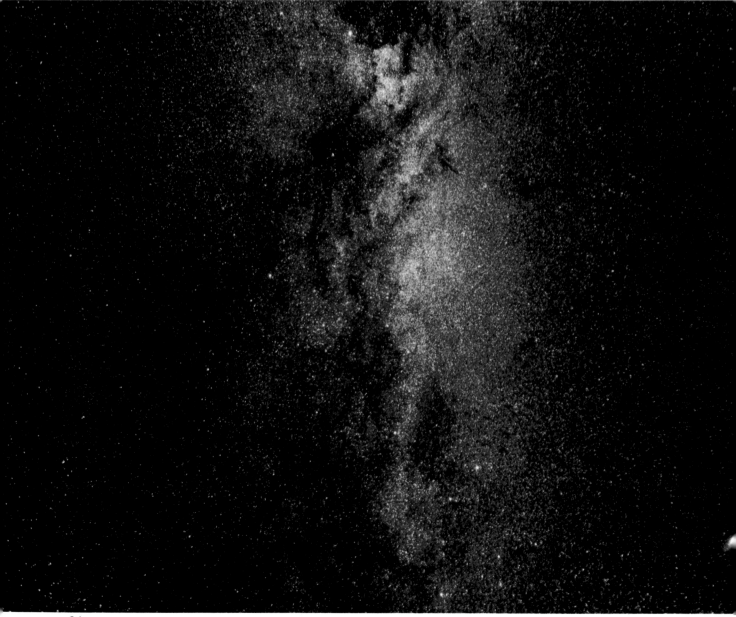

Do Stars Come in Different Shapes?

Yes. There are round stars like our sun, and stars made of gas and debris. A galaxy is a collection of a huge number of stars.

The Andromeda Constellation. It is made up of vast numbers of different kinds of stars. Our sun and earth are a very small part of the Milky Way Galaxy, which is very similar in appearance to this.

The Orion Constellation. The nebula of this huge constellation is a vast area of gas. At first the gas is illuminated by the surrounding stars and absorbs the stars' energy. Later it glows with its own light.

The Pleiades Cluster. This is also called The Seven Sisters and has thousands of stars. The lighter blue sections around the seven stars are areas of gas held together and floating in space.

● **To the Parent**

Space is full of stars in their different stages of development. Stars first form as concentrations of gaseous material, and later begin to shine like our sun. Some of the small red stars may live 10 to 200 times as long as our sun, while a few others may be 100,000 times more short-lived. In the final stages, depending mainly on type, the stars may dwindle and become small red stars, or may explode violently or implode and become those mysterious black holes.

 # What Are Comets?

(ANSWER) Comets are objects made of gas and small pieces of ice. They move around the sun but in a different way than the earth.

As a comet's orbit brings it nearer the sun, it normally grows a tail. The tail always points away from the sun because the sun's tremendous energy blows its particles outward.

What's in a Tail?

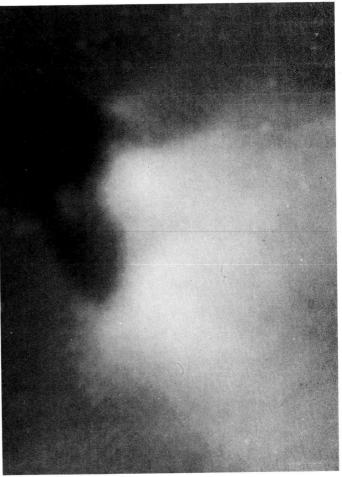

▲ Halley's Comet as it passed near the sun in 1986

■ A rare visitor

Halley's Comet takes 76 years to make a single orbit of the sun. We will not be able to see the comet again until it passes our way in the distant year 2061.

The comet's makeup

Jet

Jet

Jet

Nucleus

▲ The nucleus of Halley's Comet, above, is made up of ice and rocks, something like a dirty snowball with a rough surface. It is about 10 miles (16 km) long. Scientists believe that when it nears the sun its ice begins to vaporize. The vapor then shoots out from the Comet as is shown above and in the diagram at left. This vapor streams out behind the Comet, and appears to us as the tail.

Why Do Stars Have Names?

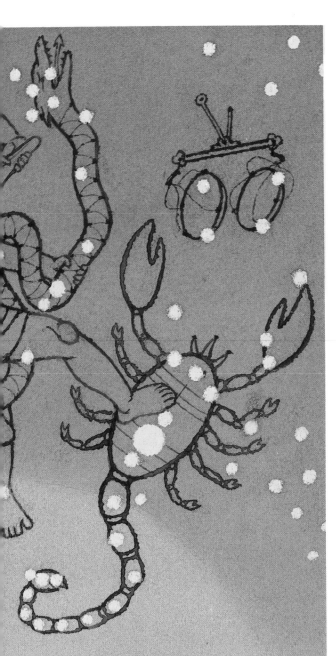

Our ancestors gave some of the stars and constellations — groups of stars — their names, calling them after the gods, animals and things they thought they looked like.

● **To the Parent**

The stars were given names by our ancestors, and these varied in different parts of the world. The names generally in use now came mostly from ancient Greece, with additions made later by other peoples. The brightest stars have their own names. Others are referred to by their constellation followed by a letter in the Greek alphabet or perhaps by a number. They are organized in descending order of brightness.

The Names of Some Stars

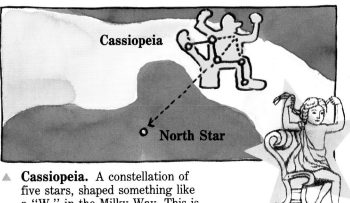

▲ **Cassiopeia.** A constellation of five stars, shaped something like a "W," in the Milky Way. This is visible in the northern sky.

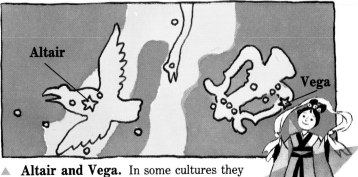

▲ **Altair and Vega.** In some cultures they are called the Weaver Maid and the Cowherd. These stars face each other from opposite sides of the Milky Way.

■ To find the North Star

The North Star is a very important star in the Northern Hemisphere because it stays in the same position and can be used for navigation. Look in the northern sky and find the Great Bear, or Big Dipper. Find the two stars near the bear's front paws. A straight line drawn through them and extended to a distance equal to five times the distance between them will bring you to the North Star. The North Star is also known as the Pole Star and Polaris.

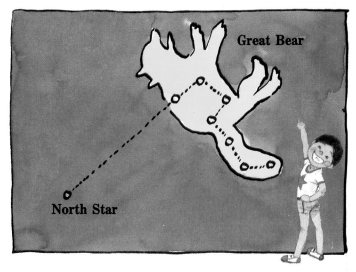

Why Don't Stars Fall From the Sky?

ANSWER Things fall to earth because the earth has a pull called gravity. Stars have a pull that is even stronger. But because stars and earth are so far apart gravity does not act in a manner to make either fall.

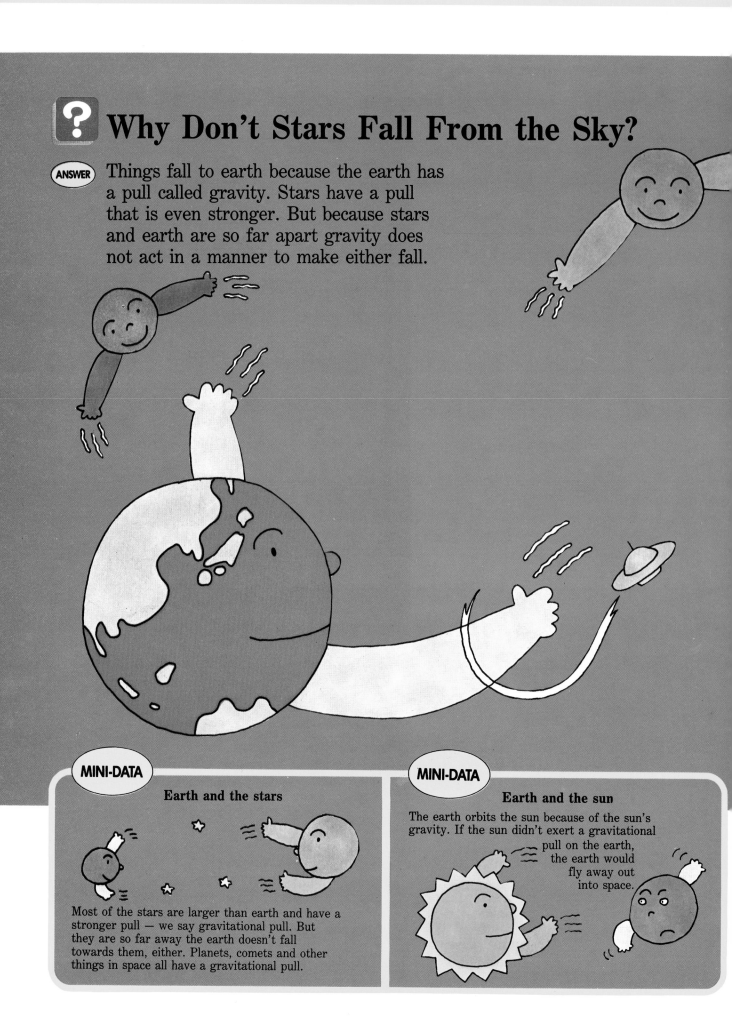

MINI-DATA

Earth and the stars

Most of the stars are larger than earth and have a stronger pull — we say gravitational pull. But they are so far away the earth doesn't fall towards them, either. Planets, comets and other things in space all have a gravitational pull.

MINI-DATA

Earth and the sun

The earth orbits the sun because of the sun's gravity. If the sun didn't exert a gravitational pull on the earth, the earth would fly away out into space.

? Why Don't People Fall Off the Earth?

The earth's gravity keeps things on its surface, or draws them back down to its surface. That's why people and buildings don't fall off the earth, and why a ball you throw up in the air comes down again.

Earth has no top, bottom or other side, since gravity holds everything on its surface. So neither we nor our friends on the other side of the world fall off.

▲ **Astronauts floating in space.** Things and people in outer space that are far away from the pull of earth's gravity can float about freely like this.

● To the Parent

Although they seem so tiny, most of the stars visible with a telescope are many times larger than earth. All celestial bodies have a gravitational pull proportional to their mass, and that of large stars is many times that of the earth. Our sun is a small star. The earth orbits the sun, but it is drawn no nearer to it because the centrifugal force generated by the earth as it follows its orbit around the sun balances exactly the gravitational pull of the sun.

Where Do Shooting Stars Go?

ANSWER Shooting stars are small particles of material that become heated as they pass through the air. They usually are burned up and disappear when they enter earth's atmosphere.

MINI-DATA

How big is a shooting star?

Usually no bigger than the head of a pin.

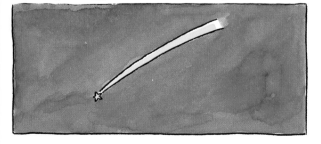

MINI-DATA

How often do they occur?

You might see about 10 in an hour.

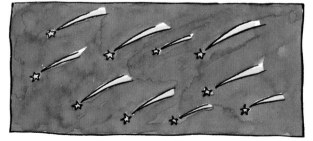

Do Larger Objects Sometimes Fall to Earth Too?

Yes, they do. Larger solid objects are called meteors. Although they also burn up with the friction of falling through the atmosphere, they don't always disappear completely. Very large meteors are rare, but when they fall, they make a noise like thunder.

▼ The Barringer Crater

It measures about 4,000 feet (1,200 m) across and 600 feet (180 m) deep. It was made by a meteor that fell to earth near Winslow, Ariz., thousands of years ago.

▲ **A meteorite section.** When it was still falling this meteorite was called a meteor and was so hot that it glowed.

What Is a UFO?

ANSWER Some people believe UFOs are spaceships that come from outer space. But nobody knows whether this is true. So far there is no proof that UFOs really do exist.

● **To the Parent**

UFO stands for unidentified flying object. It refers to things people report having seen flying in the sky but that cannot be explained. We do not know whether UFOs are really from extraterrestrial sources or not. Many UFO sightings that have been investigated are believed to have been alien space vessels, yet no physical evidence has been produced to support this. Given the conditions for life on earth, however, it is believed that a number of star systems may exist with planets capable of producing life forms somewhat similar to our own.

What UFOs might look like

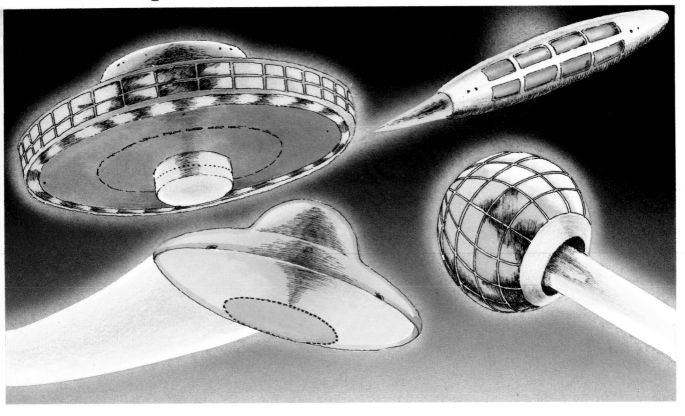

 # Is There Life on Nearby Planets?

The solar system has nine planets, including Earth. All orbit the sun. None of the other planets has life such as we have on earth because they are either too hot or too cold.

Sun

Mercury

Venus

Earth

Mars

Jupiter

Saturn

Uranus

Neptune

Pluto

Do E.T.s Exist?

ANSWER Supposed beings from space are called extraterrestrials or E.T.s for short. No one knows if they really exist. But space is unbelievably large, so it is quite possible that somewhere there are planets where such beings might be able to live.

■ Some make-believe extraterrestrials

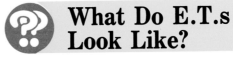

What Do E.T.s Look Like?

We don't know what they look like. People who claim to have seen an extraterrestrial have described them as looking like many different characters. Some have said such beings are about as tall as a child 10 or 11 years old.

● **To the Parent**

Along with the sightings of UFOs, some persons have also reported seeing one or more E.T.s, but so far no real evidence has turned up to confirm or deny the existence of such creatures. How one looks in the eye of the public is illustrated by the little green man in the drawing above. That may result from years of hearing about little green men from Mars. A science fiction artist imagined that E.T.s, as they came to be known in a movie, might look like the five creatures shown at left.

Since the Ground Is Flat, Then Why Is the Earth Round?

ANSWER The earth is very large, and we human beings are very small by comparison. Because we can see only a tiny part of its surface at once, it appears to us that the ground around us is flat.

A ship sailing towards us over the horizon comes into view bit by bit, starting with the top.

■ **Why we see the top first**

What Does The Earth Look Like From Outer Space?

Seen from far out in space, the earth is clearly a sphere. It seems less round from closer up.

▶ The earth as seen from outer space. It is round, as you can see.

▼ Closer up, the curve of the surface can still be seen.

A satellite photo of some Asian countries

49

? Why Does Seawater Taste Salty?

ANSWER For millions of years salt has been washed into the sea. The salt is worn away from rocks and soil by the wind and rain. Rivers carry it to the sea. The salt has nowhere else to go, so it simply stays in the ocean.

TRY THIS

We can get salt from seawater

Place a drop of seawater on a piece of black paper and let it dry. When the water evaporates, it will leave the salt behind.

MINI-DATA

Ratio of salt to seawater

If you take 3.5 ounces (100 g) of seawater and let it evaporate, you will have a bit over 0.1 ounce (3+ g) of salt left. The sample is a bit more than 3% salt.

Here Are Two Ways That We Get Salt

There are two main kinds of salt: sea salt and rock salt. Sea salt is obtained from seawater using a principle similar to the one described in Try This on the previous page.

▲ Salt fields are where salt is obtained from seawater. They are usually built right on the ocean like this one. But producing salt from seawater has become quite an expensive process.

▲ Rock salt is usually found in areas that were under the sea many thousands of years ago. In some places salt deposits are many hundreds of feet thick. They are mined, then dissolved or crushed to get the salt.

• To the Parent

The sea contains vast amounts of salt, and nobody knows how all of it got there. One theory is that a large amount was already in the seas when they were formed. It is also very likely that a fraction was carried down to the sea by running water from salt deposits in the earth. There is enough salt in all the seas of the world to cover the entire surface of the earth to a depth of 165 feet (50 m). The salt content of seas varies but is about 3.3% to 3.7% depending on location. The Dead Sea is 25% salt, and no marine life can live there.

▲ **The Dead Sea.** Things float better in water that contains a lot of salt. The water of the Dead Sea is so salty that people can float there effortlessly.

❓ Why Are There Waves?

ANSWER Waves are caused by the wind blowing and rippling up the water. The harder it blows, the bigger the waves become.

Waves during a storm. Strong winds cause very high waves. It is easy to see how high they are when they break on the shore, but waves on the open sea are also quite high.

How Do Waves Move?

If you throw a pebble into the still waters of a pond, it will cause ripples. Watch how these spread outwards making bigger and bigger circles. It looks as if the water is moving outwards, but it isn't. It's only going up and down. It's the ripples that are moving. Waves on the ocean move the same way.

● **To the Parent**

Most of the waves formed naturally are caused by the wind. Wave length is the distance from one wave peak to the next. As the wind blows, wave length increases, determining how long a wave will last. Most waves are called ripples, rollers or swells. Ripples have a very short wave length, rollers have a longer one and swells have the longest of all. Swells are old waves, no longer directly influenced by the wind, which move forward by water displacement. Waves break on the shore when they reach water that is shallower than their wave length.

Ripples on a pond. Water displacement makes it look as if the water is moving outwards.

53

❓ If All Rivers Empty Into the Sea, Why Doesn't It Overflow?

ANSWER ❶ Because some sea water is turning into vapor and rising into the air all the time.

River water comes from rain that falls from clouds. Almost all clouds are formed over the oceans from water vapor that evaporates from the sea and rises into the atmosphere.

ANSWER And because the sea is so huge there isn't enough water in the rivers to fill it up. Look at the picture. That drop on the left is all the water in all the rivers in the world. See how tiny it is compared to all the water there is in the seas.

All seas

All rivers

🤔 How Much Space Do The Oceans Cover?

If we compare the size of the world's oceans with the size of the land, we see that the oceans cover a much larger area.

▲ Lots of land on this side   ▲ Mostly ocean on this side

All the world's oceans

All the world's land

? Why Is the Sea Blue?

ANSWER The sea is blue because when sunlight strikes the surface of the water only the blue light is reflected, and all the other colors are absorbed by the water.

■ **The blue sea**

Seawater reflects only blue light. All the other colors are absorbed.

● **To the Parent**

Both the sea and the sky appear blue for the same reason. However, clear seawater absorbs light more readily than air, and all of the red, most of the violet, and four fifths of the blue has been absorbed at a depth of about 150 feet (50 m). At 360 feet (110 m) only 1% of the light remains. In turbid water along the coasts color is absorbed at even shallower depths. The sea may have a yellowish tinge if it contains much plankton.

56

What Color Is It Under Water?

t is still blue for a while,
ut color fades rapidly, and
t 500 feet (150 m) it is very
ark. At 3,300 feet (1,000 m)
here is only inky blackness.

Depth & color

Surface   ▼ A TV Tower

Ocean depths | 1,000 feet

▲ **Shallow water.** Blue light is still reflected.

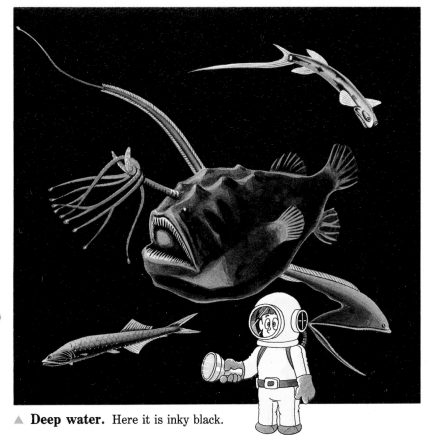

▲ **Deep water.** Here it is inky black.

How Are Coastlines Formed?

ANSWER By the action of the waves over a very long period of time.

▲ **Seal rock.** Rocks formed from harder materials often survive the pounding of the sea and become the resting places of marine animals and birds. If you look closely you may see some seals and gulls here.

● To the Parent

Our coastlines are shaped by erosion, most specifically sea erosion. Rock composition and stratification account for some of the more unusual landforms that result. The softer areas are the first to succumb to erosion, and in leaving the hard parts, create holes, blowholes, arches, pillars and other formations. In the formation we called the devil's washboard, the soft strata slanting into the sea has been washed away, leaving a stepped platform about level with the water line. The heavy seas around seal rock have worn it almost smooth.

■ **Waves wearing down rocks**

Strange Formations Cut by the Action of Waves

A row of stone pillars, the harder rocks on this coastline, are left standing after the softer parts have been eroded, or worn away by the sea.

A blowhole is more like a funnel than a hole. Water forced into it may shoot up like a fountain. Air forced through the hole can turn that water into foam.

A small island was left standing when the water eroded the softer parts of the stone and left only the hard rocks. It even has a small cap of green growing from its top.

The devil's washboard might be a good name for this, where waves have washed away softer layers of rock that used to exist between the hard layers that remain.

? How Did the Mountains Get There?

ANSWER 1 Some were formed when the earth's crust was folded.

ANSWER 2 Some formed when the crust broke and some parts jutted out.

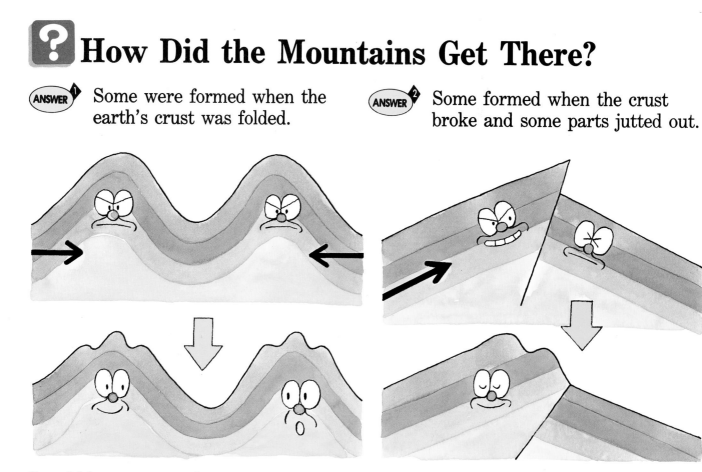

Powerful forces were at work as the rocks of the earth's crust were cooling. Pushed from both sides at once, the rocks folded up into mountains. Soil and small rocks, worn down from the peaks by wind and rain and carried down the mountain sides, formed the valley floors.

Sometimes, when the pressure from one side was greater than from the other, a layer of rock would slip and break instead of folding. Then it would ride up over the land on the other side, forming a higher mountain. The valley floors were created by debris eroded from the mountain.

▲ Mountains formed by folding are usually higher and more jagged with sharper slopes and narrower valleys.

▲ Mountains formed when the earth's crust was broken are usually lower but more massive and have wider valleys.

ANSWER 3 Mountains are formed when lava and ash are spewed onto the surface by eruption of a volcano.

Volcanic mountains are the only ones being formed now. Rock inside the earth's crust is so hot that it is liquid, or molten. Sometimes so much pressure builds up inside the earth that lava, which is molten rock, and very hot ash spew out onto the surface.

▲ Mount Fuji in Japan is an almost perfectly shaped volcano made of mainly volcanic ash and some lava.

▲ **Mount Everest.** This mountain in the Himalayas, a folded chain on the China-Nepal border, is the world's highest.

▲ **The Matterhorn.** This is a spectacular peak. Also a folded mountain, it is in the Swiss-Italian Alps.

▲ **Mount Kilimanjaro.** This peak in Africa is the world's highest volcanic mountain. It is snow-capped all year.

● To the Parent

Mountains were mainly formed in one of three ways: folding, dislocation or volcanic activity. Folding resulted in the highest and most dramatic mountain ranges: long and narrow, unbroken formations like the Himalayas of the subcontinent of India, the Alps in Europe, our own Rocky Mountains and the Andes in South America. Mount Everest reaches a height of 29,028 feet (8,800 m). The Matterhorn's highly distinctive shape is the result of glacial erosion. And Kilimanjaro, at 19,340 feet (5,895 m), is the highest peak in Africa.

Why Do Volcanoes Spit Fire?

ANSWER What looks like fire when a volcano erupts is really molten rock and ash.

▲ **Largest active crater.** Kilauea crater on Mauna Loa, a volcano on Hawaii Island, Hawaii, belches lava and ash.

Deep inside, the earth is formed of molten rock, which is called magma. In most places the earth's crust is so thick the magma cannot escape. But in others it escapes in the form of volcanoes. Magma, gas and water collect in a reservoir and, when the pressure becomes too great, force their way out onto the surface, where the magma, then called lava, becomes solid.

■ **A volcanic eruption**

Magma reservoir

Magma

Things that Come out of a Volcano

■ Gas and steam

The white smoke seen coming out of a volcano is mostly steam and other gases mixed together.

■ Volcanic ash

Sand-like particles formed when magma is blown into the air during an eruption.

▲ A close-up

■ Volcanic Bombs

Small, very hot, pieces of lava, blown high in the eruption, solidify as they fall to earth.

▲ Volcanic bomb

■ Lava

When it has cooled and hardened, lava forms pumice stone, which is full of tiny little holes.

▲ Pumice stone

Volcanic islands formed in the ocean

Sometimes a volcano forms on the seabed, and its peak rises above the surface of the water to form an island. There are many islands that were formed like this. Some of them are very old, but some are quite new.

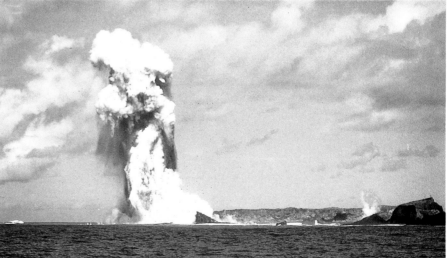

▲ A volcanic island forms, sending up a cloud of steam and gas.

What Causes Hot Springs?

ANSWER Hot springs occur where naturally hot water comes out on the surface. The water may have been heated by magma or condensed deep inside the earth from the steam in magma.

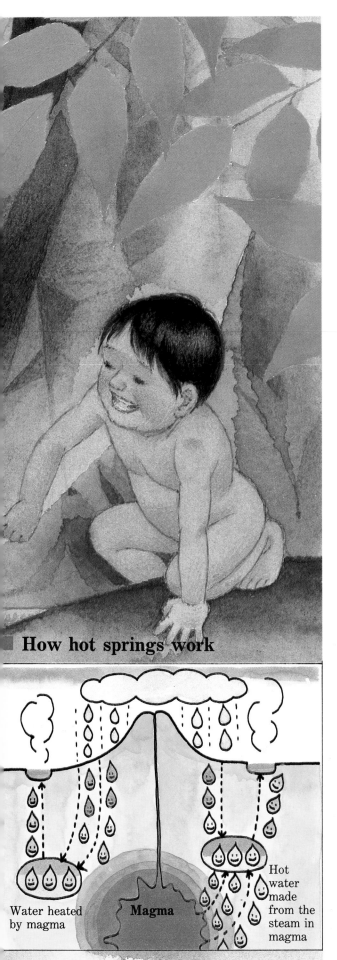

How hot springs work

Water heated by magma | **Magma** | Hot water made from the steam in magma

Two Unusual Hot Springs

▲ **Sand bathing.** To warm themselves and relax, people are buried in sand heated by steam from hot springs.

▲ **Hot and cold.** In snowy Canada a group of people enjoy a hot spring bath while across a valley another group of vacationers trudge through the snow to the ski slopes.

● **To the Parent**

Hot springs are generally found in areas of volcanic activity. The water is heated as it flows through hot igneous rocks of magma deposits. Hot-spring water is usually rich in minerals and thus is considered healthy, but the lure of hot springs lies more often in their pleasurable aspect than in a healthy one.

❓ Where and How Do Rivers Start?

Upper reaches. Rivers rise high up in the narrow valleys of tall mountains.

Hydroelectricity from a dam across a river.

■ Branches of a river

△ Small streams flowing together form a large river.

● **To the Parent**

When it rains, water drains from the high places to lower ones until enough of it gathers in a single course to constitute a stream. When many small streams flow into a single course it becomes a river. Few rivers originate in underground water, though India's Ganges rises in an ice cave.

ANSWER Rain falling on the mountains forms small streams as it naturally seeks a way to drain to lower ground. Many streams meet as they take the easiest course down the mountains, eventually joining together to form a river.

▲ River water diverted and used for irrigation.

▲ **The middle reaches.** The land is not so steep, so the river is moving more slowly and is wider. The land on the banks is more level.

▲ **Lower reaches.** This river is near the ocean.

▲ River water used for city water supplies.

❓ Why Are Riverbeds Full of Stones?

ANSWER Because rivers break up rocks in the mountains and carry them downstream.

The upper reaches of a river are steep, and the water flows very fast. Larger rocks torn off of the mountains are broken down further as the force of the water tumbles them along in the riverbed.

Carried farther along by the river's current, the stones gradually become smaller and rounder as their corners are broken off and worn away. But some large stones get carried along too.

Why Are Beaches Usually So Sandy?

Sand on the beach was either brought down by a river or made by the sea crushing loose rocks against rocks on the shore.

The river flows more gently through the lower, flatter land, so that only smaller stones, now worn into rounded pebbles, and sand and gravel are being carried along.

▲ **Sandy beaches.** Some of the sand is brought down by the rivers that flow into the sea, and some is made by sea erosion as the waves break down the rocks on the shore.

▲ **White sand.** The beaches of coral islands in the tropics are made by the sea eroding the pretty-colored shells of the tiny sea creatures that form the islands.

● **To the Parent**

In the mountains, the fast-flowing current of river water erodes rocks and carries them away downstream. Erosion is greatest when the current is swiftest — at times of heavy rain or melting snows. The rocks are further broken down by friction with the banks and the riverbed. As it moves out into the lowlands and its current slackens, the river cannot carry as much debris, and it leaves behind vast amounts, which form an alluvial plain. Finer deposits of gravel and sand may be carried farther, some eventually reaching the sea.

Why Do We Have Earthquakes?

ANSWER Let's look at Japan, a country that has a lot of earthquakes. They happen mainly because the plate that Japan rests on and the floor of the Pacific Ocean press against each other, and sometimes this causes the land to shake.

▲ A building damaged in an earthquake

■ How earthquakes happen

The floor of the Pacific is slowly pushing forward and creeping under the plate upon which Japan rests. As it does so it tries to drag the edge of the Japan plate with it.

The Japan plate doesn't want to be pushed and dragged like that. It resists, trying hard to get back to its original position, and causing smaller earthquakes or earth tremors as it does so.

If it gets pushed too far, the Japan plate may suddenly snap back to its original position. This will result in a very strong earthquake.

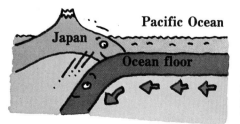

One Way to Measure the Size of an Earthquake

Intensity 0	Intensity 1	Intensity 2	Intensity 3
Can be felt only by instruments.	Some people don't notice it.	A hanging lamp sways noticeably.	A hanging lamp sways violently.

Intensity 4	Intensity 5	Intensity 6	Intensity 7
A vase of flowers will tumble over.	Stone structures fall apart.	Landslides occur.	Buildings collapse.

MINI-DATA

What people do during an earthquake

First they put out all fires. Fires can be more dangerous than the earthquake itself, so this is very important.

They are careful about running out of doors. Roof tiles or loose bricks might fall from the house and hurt them.

Inside and outside they protect their head from falling objects with something soft like a cushion or a thick pillow.

● **To the Parent**

New ocean floor is pushed constantly from the fiery depths below the crust of the earth onto the ocean floor through a rift in the crust. As this new floor hardens it joins the plates on each side of the rift and slides in both directions. As these plates drift they meet other plates, and one of them slides under the other. This grinding of the plates against each other creates motion so violent that it shakes the surface above it in what we call earthquakes.

What Makes Icebergs?

(ANSWER) Extremely large chunks of polar ice break off and fall into the sea. Icebergs are most common in spring when the ice is melting.

▲ **An Antarctic glacier.** Thick rivers of ice on land are called glaciers.

▲ **Icebergs.** Icebergs in the Arctic Ocean are usually pyramid-shaped like those here. In the Antarctic Ocean they tend to be flat on top.

How Big Are Icebergs?

Icebergs are much larger than they look because only 1/8th of them can be seen above the surface of the water. As much as seven times that amount is under the water. Really large ones can be the size of a small island. The British liner Titanic sank after colliding with one.

● To the Parent

Icebergs are huge pieces of ice that have broken off from glaciers in polar regions at the point where they meet the unfrozen sea. Arctic icebergs mostly come from the glaciers of Spitzbergen and Greenland, antarctic icebergs from the continent of Antarctica. Much floe ice frozen from seawater is also found in the Arctic Ocean. The saying "the tip of the iceberg" accurately describes the fact that seven eighths of an iceberg is beneath the surface. The sinking of the Titanic by an iceberg on its maiden voyage in 1912 claimed 1,513 lives.

TRY THIS

When ice floats in water

Test what happens when you put ice in a glass of water. You can see quite clearly that only a tiny bit of it is above the surface. Almost all of it is below the surface.

▲ **Iceberg in a glass?**

73

❓ Why Don't Trees Grow in the Desert?

(ANSWER) There are no trees in the desert because there is almost no water there, and trees need water to grow.

▲ **The Sahara.** The largest desert in the world.

▲ Little rain falls in the desert.

▲ Some countries get lots of rain.

Rain falls only rarely in the desert. When it does fall, it begins suddenly, ends as quickly and is absorbed by the sand in the wink of an eye. For this reason, it is impossible to make use of rainwater in the desert.

Does that Mean that People Can't Live in the Desert?

People are able to
live in the desert in
places called oases.
An oasis is where
water comes out of the
ground from springs. The
water fell as rain in far
distant mountains and
flowed to the oasis
underground. Trees and
plants also grow there.

Irrigation makes the
desert bloom. Water
brought over great
distances in pipes
from rivers far away
also makes it possible
for people to live in
the desert.

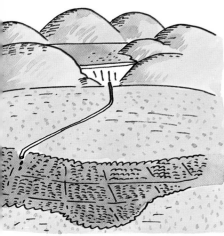

▲ **An oasis.** Springs make it possible for people to live here.

▲ **Desert agriculture.** Plants will grow only where there is water.

Why Is There Water in the Ground?

(ANSWER) Sometimes rainwater soaks into the ground and stays there.

Soil that will hold water

Soil that keeps water out

■ Types of soil

Water collects in a different way underground than it does on the surface. There are no rivers or ponds underground. Certain kinds of soil are able to absorb and hold water. Below soil like this there is always another kind of soil, one that does not absorb water. It stops the water from escaping and going deeper underground because it acts like a kind of saucer.

Soil that will hold water

Soil that keeps water out

Wells Draw on Underground Water

A well is a hole dug to a layer of soil that contains water. Water collects at the bottom of the hole and can be brought to the surface easily.

Soil that will keep water out

▶ **A desert well**

In addition to oases, deserts sometimes have other sources of water. This well in the Tunisian Sahara is a man-made one. It furnishes water for nomads who roam through the desert as well as for people who live nearby.

■ A well using natural pressure

Sometimes, if a well is dug deep enough and the location is on a slope, the water will be under pressure and come gushing out naturally. This type of well is called an artesian well, and its water flows constantly. The water is brought by rain that falls on the top of the slope.

Whee! Look, we're free! We're outside again. Yea!

Don't push so hard! You're squashing me! I'm going to have to get out of here.

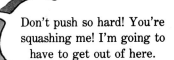

● **To the Parent**

Underground water collects in a layer of porous soil that lies above a layer of nonporous soil. So that the water will be forced up out of the ground in a spring or an artesian well, the layer of soil carrying the water must be on a slope, or the inlet from which the water originally came must be in a location higher than the place where the water gushes from its submerged source.

 What Are These?

■ Mars

Mars is Earth's neighbor and is about 1½ times as far from the sun as Earth. Earth is almost seven times as large as Mars. There is ice at Mars' poles, but it is a different ice than Earth has. Mars has many canyons and craters, some of them bigger than any found on Earth.

■ Jupiter

Jupiter, the largest planet in our solar system, is so big that 1,300 Earths could fit inside it. The planet spins so fast that its day is only 10 hours long, less than half of Earth's. It takes Jupiter 12 Earth years to travel around the sun. The white spot is one of Jupiter's moons.

■ Saturn

This is next beyond Jupiter and is the second largest planet. Pictures from the Voyager 2 spacecraft showed that Saturn has 20 moons, double the number that had been seen before. Saturn is best known for the rings that circle it. Scientists believe they are made of rocks and ice.

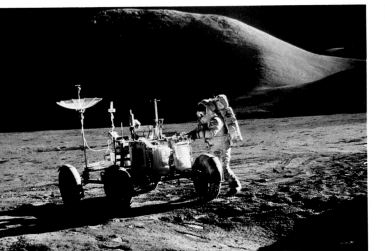

■ The moon's surface

Man first set foot on the moon in 1969. The astronauts who landed on it wore space suits and rode in an electric dune buggy called Rover. This was one of the television pictures of the landing sent back to Earth.

■ A weather satellite

This is one of a number of weather satellites launched into space by various countries to help keep track of the weather around the globe. It radios photographs of the earth's atmosphere back to earth for use in preparing weather forecasts.

▲ **A weather satellite photograph**

■ The Space Shuttle

This is a space vehicle that can go outside the earth's atmosphere into space and come back again. When it is launched it sits piggy-back on a mammoth rocket that is used and discarded. Since it can be used over and over again, the Space Shuttle will be very useful when man begins constructing space stations.

❓ And What in the World Are These?

■ An ox-bow lake of a lowland river

The larger aerial photograph above makes it clear. The ox-bow lake was once part of the river, but is now silted up and cut off from it.

■ Salt collection

Here salt is being taken out of seawater by a collector with a conveyor belt and a truck. The seawater evaporates, leaving the salt. These salt fields, the largest ones in the world, are located in Mexico.

■ Pillars carved by erosion

Sometimes when rocks in the ground are eroded, harder rocks below them remain and form pillars as shown here. Erosion has been responsible for creating some of the world's most spectacular scenery. An example is America's Grand Canyon. It was cut by the meandering Colorado River.

● **To the Parent**

The top and bottom photos are both unusual geographic features. Note that part of the ox-bow lake has been filled in. It is easy to see. If the hard top of the pillars fell off, the entire pillar might then collapse.

Growing-Up Album

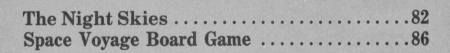

The Night Skies
The Spring Sky

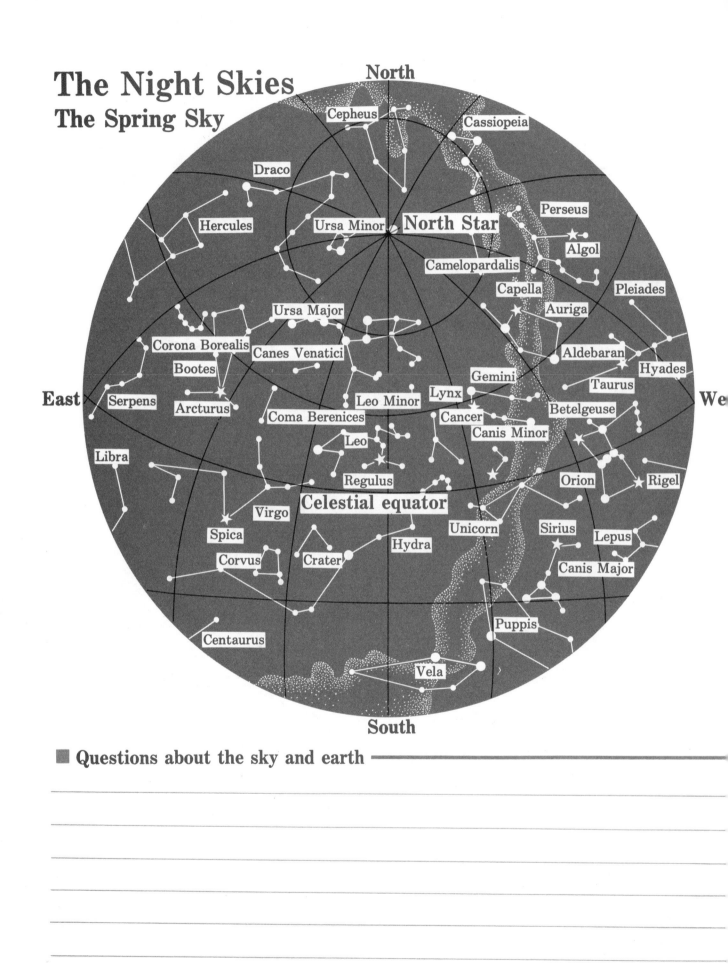

North

Cepheus

Cassiopeia

Draco

Perseus

Hercules

Ursa Minor   **North Star**

Algol

Camelopardalis

Capella   Pleiades

Auriga

Ursa Major

Corona Borealis

Aldebaran

Canes Venatici

Bootes

Hyades

Gemini   Taurus

East   Serpens

Leo Minor   Lynx

We

Arcturus

Coma Berenices   Cancer   Betelgeuse

Canis Minor

Leo

Libra

Orion   Rigel

Regulus   **Celestial equator**

Virgo   Unicorn   Sirius

Hydra   Lepus

Spica

Corvus   Crater   Canis Major

Centaurus   Puppis

Vela

South

■ Questions about the sky and earth

82

The Summer Sky

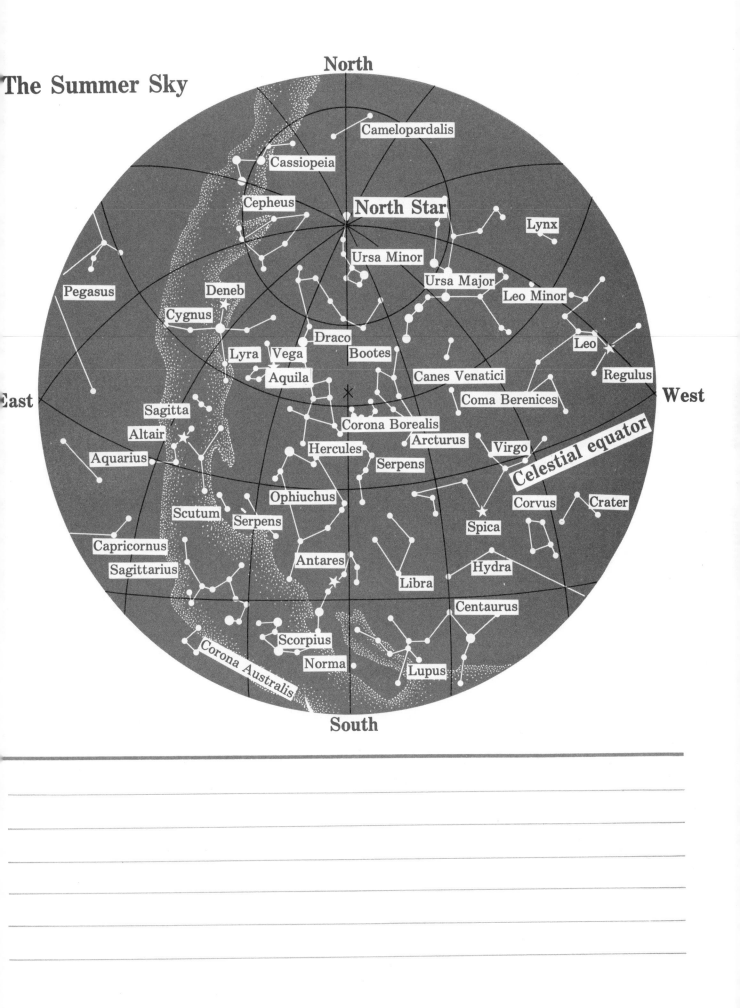

The Autumn Sky

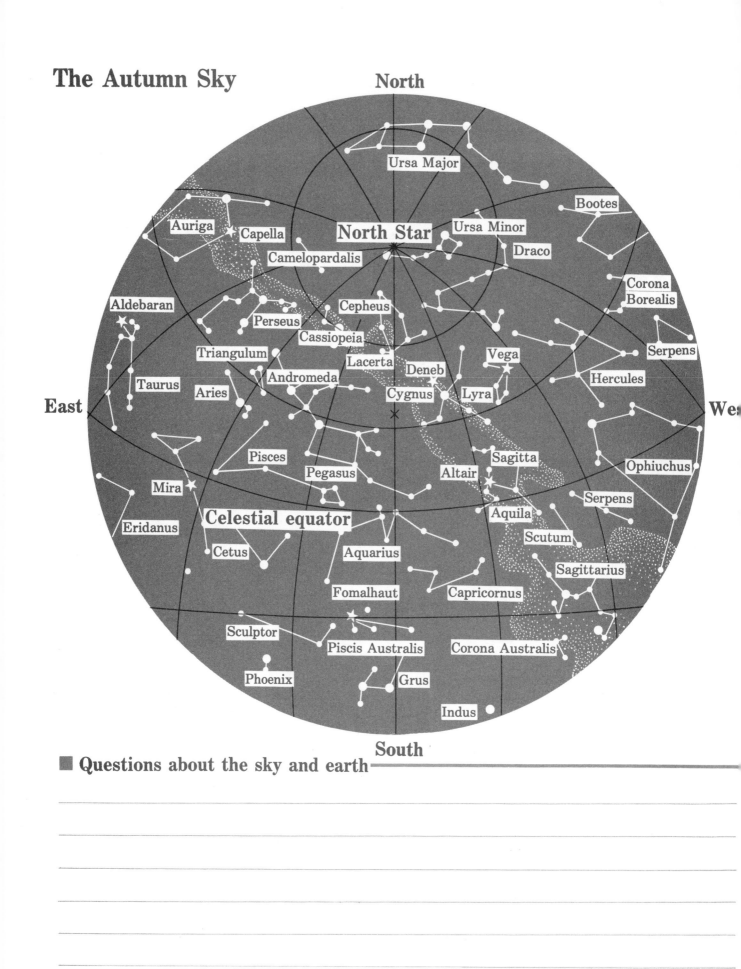

North

Ursa Major

Bootes

Auriga

Capella

North Star

Ursa Minor

Draco

Cameleopardalis

Corona Borealis

Aldebaran

Cepheus

Perseus

Cassiopeia

Vega

Serpens

Triangulum

Lacerta

Hercules

Andromeda

Deneb

East

Taurus

Cygnus

Lyra

West

Aries

Sagitta

Pisces

Ophiuchus

Mira

Pegasus

Altair

Serpens

Aquila

Celestial equator

Eridanus

Scutum

Cetus

Aquarius

Sagittarius

Fomalhaut

Capricornus

Sculptor

Piscis Australis

Corona Australis

Phoenix

Grus

Indus

South

■ Questions about the sky and earth

The Winter Sky

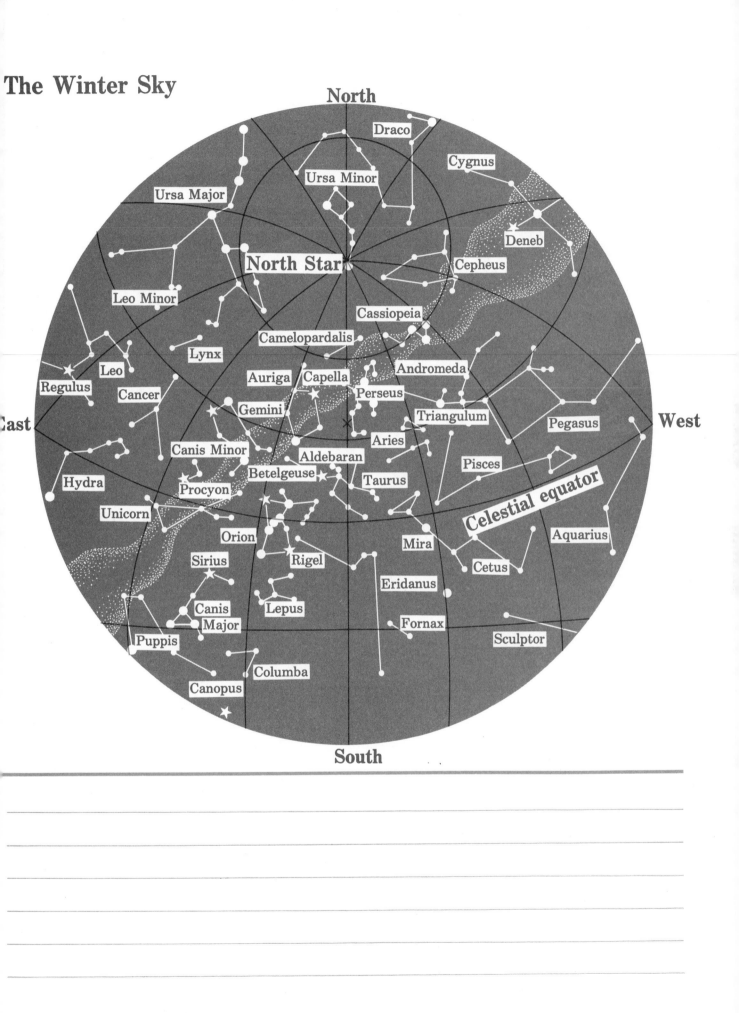

Space Voyage Board Game

Play stone, scissors, paper to advance. Stone is a fist. Scissors are two fingers extended. Paper is an open palm. Stone beats scissors. Scissors beat paper. Paper beats stone. If you win with stone, advance one. If you win with scissors, advance two. If you win with paper, advance three.

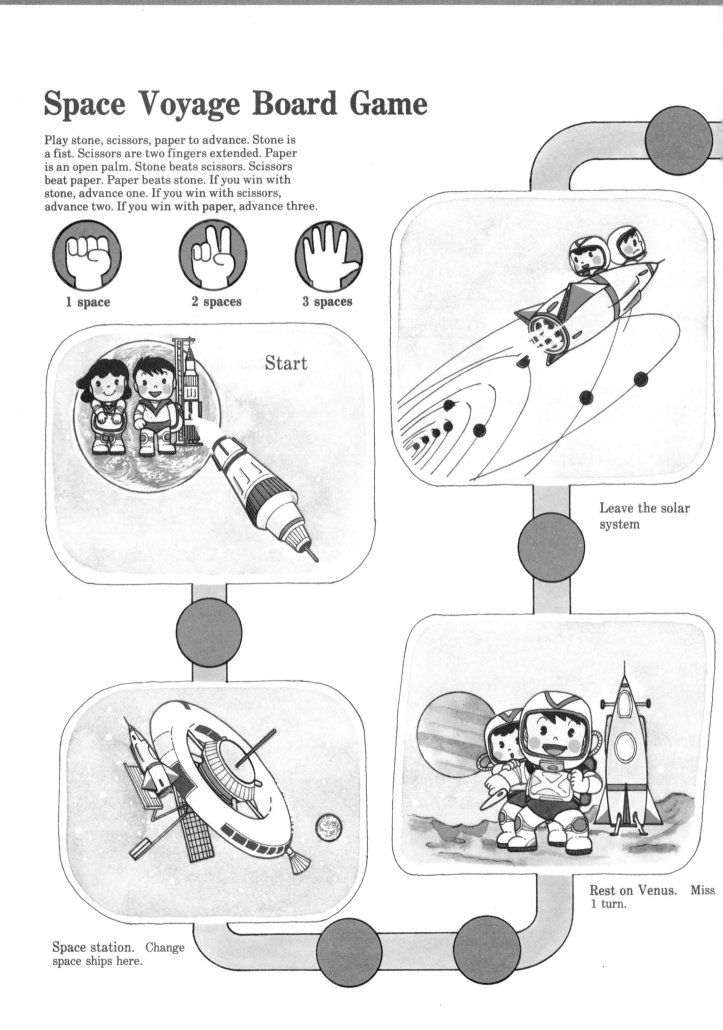

1 space

2 spaces

3 spaces

Start

Leave the solar system

Rest on Venus.   Miss 1 turn.

Space station.   Change space ships here.

Engine failure

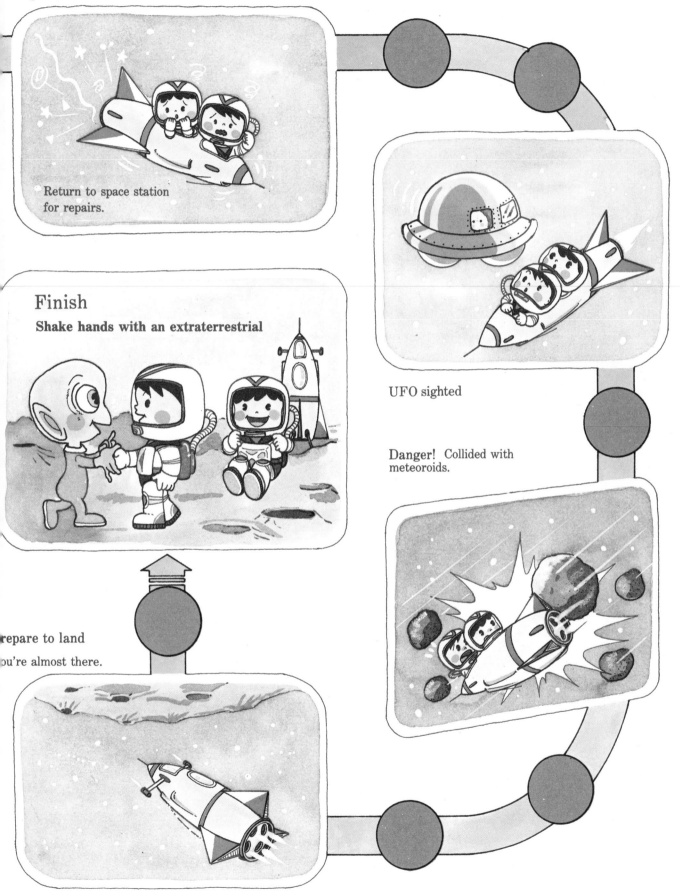

Return to space station
for repairs.

Finish

Shake hands with an extraterrestrial

UFO sighted

Danger! Collided with
meteoroids.

repare to land
ou're almost there.

A Child's First Library of Learning

Sky and Earth

TIME
LIFE ®

Time-Life Books Inc. is a wholly owned subsidiary of
Time Incorporated.
Time-Life Books, Alexandria, Virginia
Children's Publishing

Director:	Robert H. Smith
Associate Director:	R. S. Wotkyns III
Editorial Director:	Neil Kagan
Promotion Director:	Kathleen Tresnak
Editorial Consultants:	Jacqueline A. Ball
	Andrew Gutelle

Editorial Supervision by:
International Editorial Services Inc.
Tokyo, Japan

Editor:	C. E. Berry
Editorial Research:	Miki Ishii
Design:	Kim Bolitho
Writer:	Pauline Bush
Educational Consultants:	Janette Bryden
	Laurie Hanawa
Translation:	Ronald K. Jones

Library of Congress Cataloging in Publication Data
Sky and earth.
    p.   cm. — (A Child's first library of learning)
   Summary: Provides answers to questions about the seasons,
rivers, deserts, volcanoes, oceans, icebergs, moon, stars, planets,
and space. An activities section is included.
  ISBN 0-8094-4837-8.   ISBN 0-8094-4838-6 (lib. bdg.)
   1. Astronomy—Miscellanea—Juvenile literature. 2. Geophysics
—Miscellanea—Juvenile literature. [1. Geophysics—Miscellanea.
2. Earth—Miscellanea. 3. Astronomy—Miscellanea. 4. Questions
and answers.]   I. Time-Life Books.   II. Series.
QB46.S58 1988   520—dc19   88-20172
©1988 Time-Life Books Inc.
©1983 Gakken Co. Ltd.

Fourth printing 1989. Printed in U.S.A.
Published simultaneously in Canada.

TIME-LIFE is a trademark of Time Incorporated U.S.A.

Time-Life Books Inc. offers a wide range of fine publications,
including *Fraggle Rock,* a home video series. For subscription
information, call 1-800-621-7026, or write TIME-LIFE BOOKS,
P.O. Box C-32068, Richmond, Virginia 23261-2068.

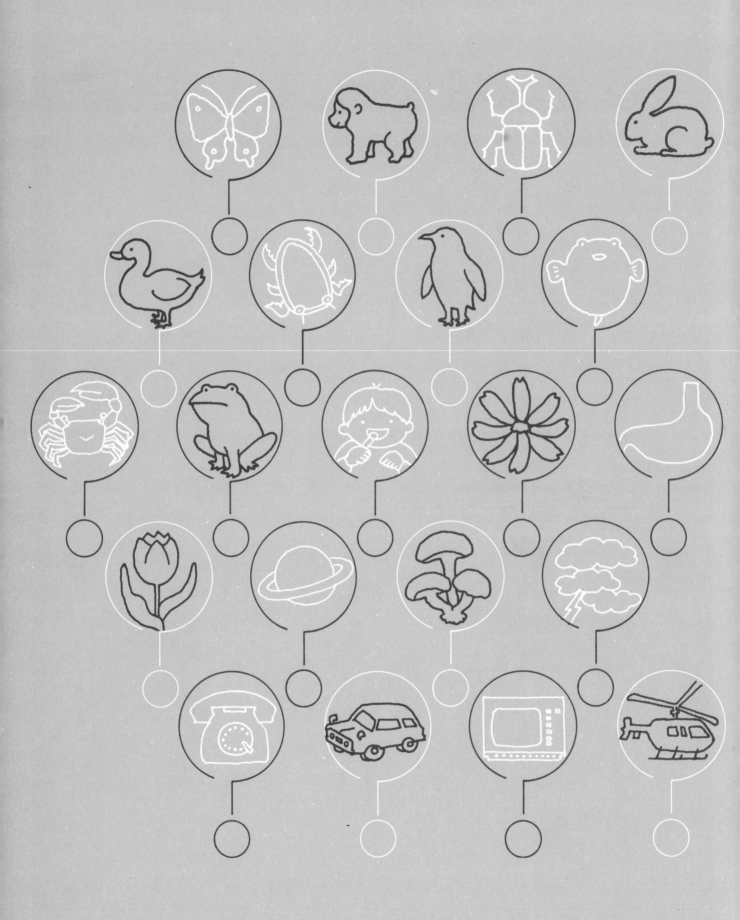